Words.

Florence Thomas

Presentation by *BookLeaf Publishing*

Web: www.bookleafpub.com

E-mail: info@bookleafpub.com

ISBN: 9789357740081

First edition 2023

For Gary

Odyssey

It begins with a question, a quest.
A lone sailor leaves the Sandy Strand
To wander in the winedark sea of the West
Leaving Gerty blooming in the sand.
These seas are heavy with naughty argonauts
Tumbling through a torrent of terabytes
Each fleeting face a precious seconds lost
In whirling vortex which agitates, numbs,
delights.
The faded banks of Lethe loom straight ahead
A silent spectator to the cacophony crashing
with cymbals cries,
The focus eaters, the glamazons, the living and
the dead,
They drift on endlessly performing for unseeing
eyes.
It's a cyber cosmos in an infinite blue Rhine,
Powered by a nameless child in a cobalt mine.

Let's move out of Midsomer.

It's a whodunnit, a mystery, a
killer-chiller-thriller
Surrounded by bodies
Every touch documented in fingerprints
And the evidence keeps on piling up.

In a pastel-hued quaint village scene,
Its dificult to spot darkness.
Until an arterial spray spreads out in a crimson
lake
Reflected, every passing bird is a red herring.

Let's move out of Midsomer.
These hushed hamlets whisper when they smile.
We can run in the night
And escape our fate.

Deadlines

Writer's block.
Chop chop
Echoing clock
Reminding of the grinding
Time pressures binding
You to this seat.

You should have started
Earlier
Shouldn't have departed
To that party
And that the other party
Ah, well.

Now the page is blank
And your bank
Is calling you about the charges
As you look down at empty margins
Waiting for a burst of linguistic largess.

Tick tock
It won't stop
The page begins to mock
A cursor flickers
Dizzy, hungover, sicker

With the ghost of stale liquor
Your breath gets quicker.

Then
Suddenly
Your life switches genres
And your story begins.

Gin & Tonic: a haiku set

Brighter than Champagne
Quinine rich but please - only
Fevertree darling

Floral, fruity, dry
Lets have fun tonight ladies
Envelope our lives

Garnish with grapefruit
Make it a double shot too
Dance til our cheer ends

Where are you going?

"And where are you going?" Said older to
younger
"That boy is trouble, will you never learn?
His heart is hidden - if ever he had one
Don't cry, don't cry, it's a valid concern.

Live a life that's memorable,
Leave your stamp upon the world,
But steady hands draw straighter lines
The tangled web of your life has barely
unfurled."

"You've never seen me" said younger to older
"You sit here unmoving and talk at the walls.
I need to grow and he's promised to go with me
I can't sit and stay in your dusty halls.

My stamp requires a steady flow of ink,
Even if its made from blood or tears
I need to go now, I can hear him outside.
I love you but I won't be cowed by your fears."

"Oh when will you learn?" Said older to older
"Your dinner grows cold and your house does
too.

You should have asked more, you should have said less,
Now your nest is empty and she won't come back to you."

The Bake-Off

I sing of the arms and of the pan,
Of brioches burnt and dreams turned dry,
Hopes turned ashen alongside a failed game pie,
I tell of the conflict finally stilled, how it all
began.

O muse, sing of the lofty judges' gaze,
Hopeful arms stretched out for a Hollywood
handshake,
Dreams crumbling like their overbaked cake,
And the cold overseers loom, sparing in their
praise.

The cold shriek of metal on metal hangs in the
air,
At last, the true flurry of conflict has begun.
Like Penelope at her spindle the caramel is spun,
A million threads linking in a croquembouche
prayer.

But now looms a technical skills test,
The time is short and nerves are frayed,
The task is impossible, the troops dismayed,
No hiding behind recipes, this will reveal the
best.

On the kitchen floor, two hands collide reaching
for the flour,
Soufflés forgotten; tender hands clasp tight,
Hearts melting butter-soft underneath the oven
light,
Their bakes fall by the wayside and soon ends
the allotted hour.

The judgement is brutal and only one may
remain,
Their love has condemned them and now they
must be parted,
He chances one last look back — and then he is
departed,
She picks up his fallen spatula and continues in
his name.

The competition is as stiff as the shiny meringue
peaks,
Tensions aided and activated by yeast cultures,
Rise and fall in hubristic bread sculptures,
As the battle rages through the weeks.

Until the final three emerge, battle-burnt and
weary,
But she still holds his spatula tight,
Wields it as her armour in this final fight,

And, alone, she is crowned the champion on Bake-Off 2023.

A self-employed saga

I cancel the class
The third little blow today
These small woes add up.

I advertise and
I feast on full days working
Until exam time.

Summer holidays
Classes completed, back to
Famine days again.

The Last Act

The globe contained on a small wooden stage
Empty spirits echo across blank spaces
Life drawn up from cold words on a page
And as she gazes, the figure of her beloved
forms before her

With each word spoken, She solidifies
Settling stronger in each spondee
Every night, she hears her soul in those lofty
cries
And burns as She blazes

Molten with desire but she dreads the climax
Each night praying for a triumph of her amour
But the scene always plays out unchanged
And her love crumples and fades out in Act Four

One night she snaps - suddenly
No forethought drives her hand
As flesh meets spirit and comes away bloody
The curtains close swiftly, this finale is final.

Dig it the

"See that, girly? Watch that doesn't stain"
Trailing royal crumbs through my domain
The young heir runs away giggling
My flashing disco lights traded for bottle feeds
and sleepless nights

Sometimes I miss the disco
The crisp certainties of champagne fizz
That buzz is still contained within me
I still know the high of commanding every eye

I plug in the hoover and out of the static fuzz
I hear those opening notes again and in an
instant I am abuzz
A dancefloor beckons from chequered lino
I still stand alone, still the Dancing Queen.

AGA: a haiku set

Induction hob snob
Its cast-iron heat seeps and stays
Warming cold fingers

Five ovens, one word
The AGA demands capital
Letters, logo shiny bright

The carbon footprint
Weighs as heavy as the hob
Old ways versus new

Ode to Oat Milk

The little black sticker atop the coffee cup lid
Denotes it as safe; free from cow and kid,
A sea of Guardians twitching,
Itching to expose a fellow commuter and
pitching
A fit as Veganuary blues pull taunt nerves tight.
But in these dairy-free days, one star remains
bright.
The morning cuppa, your pick-me-up cup,
The antidote to shock, sleepiness, a savage
breakup.
You won't give in to temptation, won't bow dow
to cow;
Instead you turn to oat milk now.
Less a substitute, more a saviour,
The opalescent oat drink has even shifted your
behaviour,
Meat-free Mondays are in, there is even talk of a
fun-run,
Still, you won't be giving up cheese for anyone.

Write

There is a power in poetry
A murky heat which lurks beneath ordinary
turns
Of phrase and elevates
Into new shapes, new
Sounds, new meanings
And gives again.

The rocket's plea

Light me up
Let me blaze in splendid majesty
Before I lose heat
And urgency
And begin to grow cold

Household Management

The muddy boot tracked through an empty hall
May be easily beaten back by tireless strokes of
the parlourmaid.
A smash leaves sharp stalactites standing in an
empty pane
Swiftly disposed of by a passing footman.

The class system was built for this.
You make your messes and in return
Outsiders track their dirt into this house
Where we stand with brushes in hand and sweep
it under the carpet.

So when you next rise up and fight the power
Pick your surroundings considerately
A crime committed in a country house has
No regard for the stress it places on the staff.

The Woes of Public Transport

A crackly announcement blares from old
speakers,
"The 7.36 service will arrive at 7.48."
The masses shudder and stamp impatient feet
But it's Britain - of course the train will be late.

Inside, the carriage reveals rows of lurid thrones,
Like a jester's hat alternating hypothermic and
arterial,
But equally itchy for the commuters locked in
close proximity,
And, of course, the gentleman next to you will
begin to eat cereal.

A young face opposite framed by black rodetes,
Unconnected to their phone, they radiate a tinny
techno beat,
The carriage turns, unified by hatred
As the youth settles unbothered in their seat.

This is the rush hour; a thousand individual
quests
Jostling and bustling, they snore and sweat and
scheme
But there is nothing to be done til Euston
So we sit and watch the steady stream.

Estoy

Yo soy: I am
Yo estoy: I am temporarily

No child feels the touch of Clotho
Busy hurtling headlong through life
In a cacophony of colour and sound
Swift-footed and sleekit
I screamed and laughed and shone with
Opportunity, possibility, wide open paths
Curled tight in each conch-curled fist
A button, a Barbie, a blood red thread and the
press of doves wings a breath on my neck and
Everything was certain and yo soy.

With each new strand interwoven
More shades, more strands, more shadow
A pattern forms — in increments
Now a hesitant weaver
Agonising over each new twist
As the threads spin on uncaring
And for the first time: feeling
The ghostly press of a gold blade
And suddenly yo estoy.

In the face of Spanish grammar proclamations

Descartes' certainty crumples like the withered
face of a rotten fruit.
Too soon the pattern is spun
Tangled up in our own thread
And the further the pattern unfolds
The clearer it becomes
someone else has the weaver this whole time.

And all around me, everything writhing,
shifting, breathing, and in the middle it's me and
yo estoy.

Dance with me

I scroll, I swipe, I tap-tap-tap
The comfort of my for you page
More familiar than my cold plastic home
Tailored exactly to who I want to be
No exclusions, it invites me in
To gaze anew at the same things

There is some fluctuation
The algorithm dances constantly
A soft samba sway of suggestions
Tantalise
All tailored to me
A lord of my virtual domain

They say we are isolated -
Disconnected from our fellow man
But I've never known a closer connection
Eat, play, get ready, go to sleep with me
Live with me
And only in the constant cha-cha of content
Am I content

In your shoes

To walk a mile in your shoes wouldn't be too
bad.
To feel the soles you've worn down press against
me
To be rubbed by rough stitches you have itched
at,
To carry your weight on me, pressing into me.
I can think of many worse things.

www.ingramcontent.com/pod-product-compliance
Lightning Source LLC
Chambersburg PA
CBHW070735160726
48003CB00006BA/2523